WOLF STORY

by

Drew Gomber

Based on the life of my 9 year companion, Laz, a gray wolf-cross breed with more wolf than 'mute.

Published in cooperation with the Author
PricePoint Publications

pricepointcreative.com

ACKNOWLEDGEMENTS

There are many people and entities I would like to thank in bringing the story of Lazarus to the printed page. First, Dianne Stallings of the Ruidoso News, who found the baby Laz wandering in Ruidoso, sick and frightened. If not for Dianne getting the little fellow to Warren Franklin, DVM, on that very day, he would not have survived.

I would also like to thank virtually everyone who handled him over the years for their patience and courage. Ira Rabke and Cille Dickinson, two of my neighbors in Lincoln, were always available to "wolf-sit" when I was out of town. They knew that in entering my home they were also entering a wolf's lair and while Laz was always friendly toward humans (as long as they didn't do anything foolish), if something had set him off, they would never have gotten out alive. And yet they, and others who I am undoubtedly forgetting to mention, returned time and time again to freshen his water and feed him over the years.

I would like to thank my parents, Ann Gomber and the late John F. Gomber, animal lovers extraordinaire who instilled in me, not only a love of God's creatures, but an abiding respect for them as well.

Gene Mazza has been a good friend and has been extremely helpful with his computer savvy and a willingness to help me even though there was no paycheck waiting for him at the end of the day. It was Gene who put together the initial draft of the story of Lazarus, adding photos and invaluable suggestions.

INTRODUCTION

There have been millions of words written about wolves. Man's fascination with them has continued unabated for centuries. It is a sad state of affairs that they have been hunted nearly to extinction and are still being fought over by extremists today. Most ranchers suffer from an almost superstitious dread of them and act as though one wolf can and will decimate a herd of a hundred cattle in one evening. The other side of that coin is the "preservationists" who are still struggling to re-introduce the wolf to the Continental United States. Both sides are passionate in their beliefs and in my opinion, both sides are wrong.

The only time that wolves kill indiscriminately is when the pack becomes too big, and when that happens, they kill everything they come across. Luckily for anything that might be in their path, that does not happen often. One of the reasons that coyotes have proliferated as they have, becoming the most successful predators on Earth, is because of man's slaughter of the wolves. To a great extent it was the wolves who kept the coyotes in check. While the uninformed seem to think that wolves are just larger versions of coyotes, the fact is that they are not – wolves EAT coyotes.

Those who fight for reintroduction are doing the wolves a disservice also. The fact that most farmers and ranchers are going to shoot them on-sight, regardless of legislation, does not seem to occur to those who consider themselves to be pro-wolf. And frequently, those who do the reintroductions seem unable to restrain themselves from petting the animal before releasing it into the wild. All that accomplishes is possibly removing any fear of man that the animal had. And to introduce wolves that are lacking that fear is foolish in the extreme. It is simply NOT WISE to remove a fear of man from one of the mightiest predators that ever walked the North American continent.

In the end, there is no longer a place for wolves in the Continental United States. It is unfair to the animals, regardless of the extreme views of those who hate them and those who think they love them. To attempt to reintroduce them into the United States merely condemns the wolves themselves.

My personal meeting with Lazarus was by chance – right place, right time, and that was all there was to it. I was lucky, too. He had a naturally sweet nature and loved me as though I were the alpha leader of his pack, which is the primary reason that I lived to tell his tale. Wolves are not housepets. They are wild animals and wild animals do not belong in the home. For those naieve enough to think that they can be domesticated, think again. Wolves have not changed in 20,000 years. They are the perfect predator and their minds are not the minds of dogs. They absolutely cannot be domesticated. The most you can hope for is that the animals will accept your presence as a pack member. If they do not completely accept you, remember this: as long as you are playing with them, they consider you to be a playmate. The second you fall or they knock you down, in the blink of an eye you go from playmate to prey.

In short, do NOT read this and go out looking for your own pet wolf. They are magnificent creatures who deserve our respect and their own privacy. Lazarus was a fluke. I will never again keep another wolf. I believe that after all the mistakes I made with him, for which he did not force me to pay with my life, my number is up at this point. I will always love them and want to view them, but from afar.

LAZARUS

As I begin to write this, he has been gone less than a week. He died Thursday, September 2, 2004, at 12:12 in the afternoon. Never had I connected with another living creature the way I connected with him and never did I love anyone or anything so much.

All of which is kind of funny, or I guess it would be to some people, when you consider that he was a creature that Man has feared since the dawn of history. A creature almost universally presented as an evil entity, a creature vastly misunderstood. He was a Gray Wolf. Despite the approximately 1/16 malamute blood that flowed through his veins, he looked and acted almost exclusively like a wolf.

Nevertheless, he lived in my home for over nine years, usually sleeping next to my bed and he never so much as scratched me. The same could not be said of several unwise folks who did things they shouldn't in front of him, and, as far as he was concerned, *to* him. Unlike dogs, a wolf will not wait to be sure whether or not your intentions are good. If you were to give him the slightest reason to distrust you, you could end up as lunch.

And then there were the coyotes… and therein lies one of many tales.

DIANNE

Lazarus, the Wolf, had three homes in his life. The first was with Ruidoso News Reporter Dianne Stallings, who found him in the parking lot behind the newspaper where he had been dumped. There used to be a breeder of hybrid wolves who lived in Ruidoso and undoubtedly this person didn't want to pay the veterinarian bills. It is also probable that Laz had far too much wolf blood in his veins, that he was, in fact, a mistake.

The tiny little fellow, who didn't weigh more than 10 pounds, was very ill with the dreaded canine disease, "parvo." Had Dianne not gotten him to a veterinarian immediately, he would not have survived. Hence, his name. The irony is that the breeder probably could have gotten a fortune for what turned out to be a magnificent specimen of a Gray Wolf, had she not so heartlessly dumped him and left him to his fate, which would have been a terrible, painful death.

Dianne kept him until he was about 6 months of age. That first cold day that she had brought him into the newspaper offices, he trembled and whimpered as he clutched desperately to her. To my knowledge, it was the last time he EVER trembled or whimpered, but he sure created a poignant picture that day. After that, the transformation was nothing short of incredible.

As Lazarus recovered his health, he began to grow so fast that you could almost HEAR his bones enlarging. People who would see him each week would, nevertheless, exclaim in amazement "*that's* Lazarus??"

We theorized that perhaps Dianne was switching out the animals, substituting one that was twice the size of the one she had showed us the previous week. Of course, we were just being silly, but it illustrates how fast he was growing. At six months, Lazarus was a hundred pounds.

Dianne was wise in her treatment of Lazarus, and I have a strong suspicion that in a very real way, I owe my life to her. She was determined that he be a "good boy" and therefore, understanding his lineage, she would daily knock him over on his side, get down on all fours, hold him down and growl at him. In this way, he understood that she was dominant. If this sort of feeling is not instilled in the animal at an early age, there is a chance that it never will be.

Had she not done this when he was small enough to allow it, he could have become extremely dangerous by the time I got him. Luckily, in addition to this treatment, it helped that he really did have a sweet and fun-loving nature. But there was no getting around the fact that he was a wolf, and by the time he was six months, thanks to Dianne, he was well-acclimated to people.

And, by that time, he was getting to be a bit of a handful for Dianne. She still brought him to the office, where he would rush from desk to desk and workplace to workplace, wildly greeting those he considered his personal friends. Dianne, who is about five feet tall, just flew around behind him on the other end of the leash. I was constantly reminded of a kite…

The last straw for Dianne was the day she left him in her car behind the newspaper offices. Laz got bored, as all youngsters tend to do, and, alleviated his boredom by eating Dianne's steering wheel.

It was about that time, in June of 1995, that I was relocating to a home in Bent, New Mexico, which had six or seven acres to go with it. Dianne approached me and asked if it would be possible for me to take Laz off of her hands, as she already had too many pets, anyway.

I was more than happy to do it. The very first toy I ever had was a ceramic wolf that my Mom had let me play with as a child. For some reason, I had always felt an affinity for lupines. Many others have told me that they have felt the same way, so I guess it's a fairly common fantasy.

And a fantasy is what it is. I was to learn over the next nine years that despite what many people seem to think, wolves are not just some kind of wild dog. They are more like some kind of "Superdog." And believe me, you *do not* want an animal like this tracking you in the wild, to say nothing of actually having one in your home. They are beautiful, but if you presume to treat them like a big, beautiful dog, chances are they will kill you the first time you attempt to discipline them.

Initially, Lazarus didn't even care to be petted. He would jerk his head away when I reached for him, as though he suspected that I might be about to grab him. (Actually, I realized later that I was lucky he didn't bite me). Eventually, he decided that petting was pretty cool, all things considered. One thing he *never* minded was having his tail pulled. While he did not care to be touched on the head, he absolutely loved being led around backwards by his tail! Go figure.

Wolves are predators, of course, and tend to see many things that we humans do as being aggressive, whether that is the case or not. Of course, unlike Man – the ultimate predator – wolves never kill for no reason. It is always for self-defense, food or territory – hunting ground, if you will.

It is almost as if Man – the destroyer of wolves – is destroying them out of envy. Their society is so much more, well, *civilized* than ours. There are no orphans in a wolf pack. If the parents are killed, the pack raises the babies. They mate for life and they care for one another to the end. In a very real sense it is *we* who are the savages.

When I moved into the house in Bent, I already had another dog and two cats, all of whom were a source of some concern when I realized that the animal I was bringing to live with them might just consider them to be prey.

I made a point of having Dianne bring Laz over at the same time that I came with Roxanne, my Lab/Dobie mix, so that they both arrived simultaneously and could not get territorial. It was probably unnecessary. Laz immediately gravitated to Roxanne as he would to an older sibling. Of course, he towered over her, but always showed respect to her. As Rox got older and crankier, she would occasionally snap at him. He would wag his tail and move off. He was not afraid, he was just respectful. I always appreciated that, but whether or not Roxanne did is another story.

Of Wives and Wolves

I was still married when I first moved to Bent, and my wife felt that I should be "disciplining" Laz, and "training" him. Try as I did to make her understand that you simply can't train a wild animal, she remained obstinate in her opinion. Finally, she began telling our friends that "Drew is the master, but I'm the disciplinarian." All I could do was sigh heavily and see how it worked out.

One day I walked through the living room to see her "spanking" Lazarus. She was hitting him on the rump as hard as she could with her open hand as he stood there. To be fair, she wasn't trying to hurt him. She wasn't a bad person, and with her open palm, she thought that she was "humanely" disciplining him. Laz, however, thought she was petting him – he looked at me happily as I passed by and I noticed that his tail was wagging. I grinned to myself and said nothing as I went into the bedroom.

A few minutes later, a rather resounding silence began emanating from the living room. Just as I was about to go investigate, my wife came in and sat heavily down on the bed. She was ashen.

Shaking her head, she said that "I guess you were right after all. He moved faster than a snake. I was hitting him and he suddenly reached around behind him and grabbed me by the arm. I've never seen anything move so fast."

It was easy to put together what had happened. Laz had turned toward her, thinking she was petting him, and saw – or heard – the aggression either on her face or in her voice, or both. He didn't want to hurt her. He had simply stopped her. He never was vindictive, the evidence being that as soon as she stopped, he released her and walked off.

She never again tried to "discipline" him.

However, while she was *never* cruel to animals, there is no doubt in my mind that she must have yearned to introduce him to *some* discipline, so it must have been terribly frustrating for her. At one point in 1996, my sister was visiting us in Bent. I was at work one evening, leaving my sister, Susan Hallock, at home with my wife, passing the time talking and watching television.

My wife had always been an avid chewer of gum and bought it in those large economy packages. On this particular night, Susan and my wife were seated on the couch in the living room, chatting. Laz was making himself obnoxious, at least as far as my wife was concerned, with his usual "What's this??" approach to virtually everything. On a number of occasions, he had grabbed her beer off of the long table in front of the couch (what's *this*??), and drank it from the can. He accomplished this by tilting it and adding instantaneous new holes, spraying beer into his mouth – and everywhere else. None of this had endeared him to the Little Woman.

He *had* developed a taste for beer though. At one point, we actually gave it to him in the hopes that it might calm down his more-or-less demented demeanor. As you have no doubt already deduced, this was not the brightest idea either of us had ever had. Does one really want a humongous, drunken wolf in one's home?

While they were seated on the couch, my wife had taken her package of gum and placed it on the back of the couch. Neither woman was aware of the fact that Laz had even noticed this.

Finally, it was decided that Laz would be banished to the outside (he was still running loose at this point) until I got home. My sister remained on the couch, while my wife got up, walked over to the door and informed Laz that he was being evicted.

He waited until she opened the door and then went into action. Vaulting over the long, low table in front of the couch, he leaped right up next to Susan, grabbed the package of gum and then raced out the front door. He did this so fast that both women were left wondering what had just happened until they saw him with the gum outside and realized that it was no longer on the couch. My sister is still laughing about it, although I don't know whether or not that is the case with my ex-wife.

LAZ ELECTS TO STAY

In the beginning, I just let him run free, which was the first of many stupid mistakes that I made dealing with Lazarus. He generally stayed around the house, but as time passed and the weeks became months, he began to enlarge the more or less circular area that he considered to be his territory.

On one occasion, he frightened one of my neighbors badly when he stepped out of the brush a few feet in front of the fellow. The poor guy didn't know if Lazarus was a wild one or not. Ranchers have an almost superstitious fear of wolves and will shoot them on sight. Luckily, my neighbor was not armed, or Laz would probably have died – another victim of man's primordial fear of the wolf.

But even *that* wasn't enough to make me stop and think. What it took was the day I returned from checking the mail to find that Laz was gone. I had only been gone a few minutes, but Laz was nowhere to be found. Finally, I glimpsed him, about a quarter mile away, walking to the top of a ridgeline. I knew that on the other side of that ridgeline was a hundred miles of wilderness and then Mexico, and it made me suddenly nervous.

I called out to him and he stopped and turned to look in my direction. As I implored him to come back, he turned and looked at the ridgeline, then back at me, then back at the ridgeline. He did this several more times and then slowly turned and began trotting back toward me. I knew, at that moment, that had he crossed that ridgeline, I would never have seen him again. He was headed for the wild, but made a conscious decision to stay with me. It was a compliment, the magnitude of which I would not realize for several more years.

OF HORSES AND APPLES

I don't believe that, in his entire life, Lazarus was ever afraid of any man or beast. But there was *one* time when he got his butt kicked.

I had been giving some apples to the horses boarding on my property and Laz beheld a nice, big, red juicy apple – in one of the horse's mouths. He came at the mare from the side, at a dead run and, sailing through the air, snatched the apple right out of her mouth without touching her. His mistake was to then stop, wag his tail, and see what the horse would do. Well, for once, Laz had underestimated another animal and that horse proceeded to stomp the living crap out of him. I ran at her, waving my hat, and she moved off. Laz leapt to his feet and ran to the house, where he stood, holding one of his hind paws in the air, with a kind of "What happened?" look on his face.

I VERY carefully examined him for injuries. I didn't want to suddenly cause him any pain, especially when his face was six inches from mine. The only thing I found was that one of the toes on his left hind leg had been broken. Other than that, he was fine. I supposed that should have taught him a lesson and put some fear of horses into him, but noooooooooo…

After the incident where Laz had almost vanished into the wild, I converted an old goat pen into a place for him, but hated to put him in it, because it made him *feel* alone, and wolves are animals that prefer pack conditions.

THE BOOBY TRAP

Perhaps it was boredom that made him perpetrate what I always considered to be his greatest crime against humanity – "humanity" being in the form of yours truly.

I had been worried that Laz might dig his way out underneath the gate of the pen, which was the only part of the fencing that wasn't buried in the ground. Therefore, I placed four concrete blocks in stacks of two just inside the gate (which opened outwardly) and hoped that would suffice.

One night, I returned home from work around midnight, and as I strolled up to the pen, I couldn't help but notice that instead of his usual joyous leaping about, Laz was just sitting there, watching me. I didn't know it, but the show was about to begin. And I was to be the star!

I opened the gate and, instead of rushing down the hillside to the house, as was his custom, Laz leaped over the blocks and once he was outside the pen, sat down and continued to watch me. I didn't think anything of it – at the time.

Spying Laz's dinner dish on the other side of the pen, I took the bait. Stepping over the concrete blocks to go and get it, I stepped down on the other side. In the darkness, my foot kept going down, and down, and down. Too late, I realized that he had dug a hole – no, it was more like a trench – no, in actual point of fact, it was so deep that I think he may have been on his way to China.

Naturally, I lost my balance and toppled into his little booby trap. I looked back up at the concrete blocks from my new vantage point at the bottom of the hole, just in time to see Laz lean over them, and with his chest, push one in on top of me. (The whole time, he had a look on his face that said "Isn't this fun?")

Then, he ran down the hillside in high spirits, and waited for me at the house. Despite the fact that I had to drag myself down there, practically on my belly, it was just too funny not to laugh. It was not as though he was a pet. He was more like a roomie – a buddy, playing practical jokes on me. Eventually, of course, he became something much more – like a brother.

But he was still a lonely animal, games aside, and he truly needed some other canine, besides the elderly Roxanne, to keep him company.

And that was when Blanche rather conveniently showed up.

BLANCHE

Her name wasn't Blanche at the time, of course. One day in October of 1995, I was standing in my back yard, preparing to head into work at the Ruidoso News, when a car suddenly appeared at the top of the rise that was my driveway. This driveway was such that one abruptly topped a rise to find oneself already in the backyard, and it was only then that one could tell if anyone was home or not. To turn around, one had to drive all the way down to the house.

Also, the house had been abandoned for six years before I moved in. It was clear that the driver of the car was not prepared for someone to be present. He stopped and got out, explaining to me that he had been under the impression that the place was still vacant and that he was there to do a little dog a favor.

A favor? I wondered what *this* meant. I didn't have to wonder long. This fellow went on to explain that he had this little dog with him that was being abused by the son of the woman he lived with on the Mescalero Reservation. He claimed that the little dog was being used as bait to "train" a Pit Bull to kill. This fool's solution was to take this small, inoffensive little dog, who he called "Kiwi" and who was clearly desperate to find a home and love, and leave her at an abandoned house with some food and water.

A true humanitarian. What did he think would happen when the food and water ran out, assuming the little critter hadn't already been killed by coyotes or mountain lions? I took her, if for no other reason, than to get her away from this moron – and I hope he reads this, if he can read at all.

She was – and is – only about 15 pounds. She is a cross between – get this – a Pomeranian and a Chow-chow. She is orange in color with the Pom face and a little rotund body to go with it. As a friend of mine once put it, she "hones her cuteness to a fine edge."

It was weeks before her little tail came out from between her legs and she began to realize that yes, she had found a real home at last. The guy had said she was a year old which made her about the same age as Laz. I thought "Great. A playmate." But it wasn't that easy.

After renaming the little mutt Blanche duBois (like the character in "Streetcar Named Desire" she "relies on the kindness of strangers") I couldn't help but notice that she wasn't overly anxious to get too close to Laz, who was *very* curious about her.

After a few days, she began to walk with me up to his pen and touch noses with him through the wire. So far, at least, they seemed to be getting along fine. Finally, I decided that I would let him out and see what happened.

Well, touching noses through a fence was one thing, but having this Behemoth suddenly in her face was quite a different story. As I unlocked the cage, and she realized what I was doing, Blanche's little eyes turned into saucers. Shrieking in terror (she undoubtedly thought that I was going to feed her to this monster), she wheeled and took off for the house at the approximate speed of light. I tried to close the half-opened gate, but it was too late.

"Dogzilla," as he was occasionally known, pushed past me, knocking me down, and took off after Blanche. What I had done, essentially, was the same thing as throwing a spool of thread out in front of a kitten…

There wasn't a whole lot I could do other than stand and watch. Blanche began circling the house as fast as her little legs would carry her. In the long stretches, he would begin to gain on her, but she could corner better than him. It was not unlike watching a semi-trailer pursue a Volkswagon Beetle.

Finally, I went in the back door, walked through the house and opened the front door. On the next pass, I called to Blanche, and she immediately cut and ran through the front door, which I quickly closed behind her. As soon as I did, the door reverberated with a dull thud as Laz slammed into it.

The next day, they met quite accidentally at the back door and all was fine. The two began a tentative friendship that was destined to be life-long. But not before it was cemented by adversity, in the form of some coyotes wanting to eat Blanche. They regretted that choice of prey for the rest of their lives – both seconds of them. But I'm getting ahead of myself.

It had worked out well. Laz now had something of a "pack" for himself. He acknowledged me as the Alpha – the proof of that is that I am alive to write this – and he was second in command. Then came my other cat Mr. Jazz, then Blanche and at the bottom of the ladder was Fred, a sweet and inoffensive little kitty. Roxanne served as a sort of aloof matriarch, above all the petty problems of the others, until her death in 1999.

Rox was a good-natured dog, who to me, holds her own place in the annals of sweet and humorous dog stories. She had been abused as a puppy and preferred to spend all her time strictly with me, who she knew she could trust. When I wasn't around, she preferred to spend all her time strictly on the couch, where she knew she would be comfortable. Of course, knowing the household illegality of her being on the couch, she always waited until all the humans had left the room. She never did figure out that we could hear the thing squeak when she got onto it from the other room. But this story is not about Roxanne…

Fred Astaire Gomber is a sweet, "Sylvester"-look-alike black and white kitty who is shy and retiring. Fred's idea of an exciting day is to follow a patch of sun around the room. In 1995, he was three. Unlike most cats, Fred liked everyone – even mice. Oh sure, he would catch them. But then he would free them! "Run, my brothers, run" he would say, "the giant is approaching!"

While this was quite the humanitarian approach, at least where Fred was concerned, it was leading to something of a rodent problem. Laz enjoyed eating them, but seemed to feel that hunting them was somewhat beneath him.

Mr. Jazz

When I had first come to New Mexico from Florida, I let my cats outside, not realizing the danger I was placing them in here in the mountains. New Mexico is full of predators. When I arrived in The Land of Enchantment, I had two cats – Fred and Mr. Prescott Jazz (I should point out here that my then-teenaged stepdaughter, Randi, had named them both). Jazzy fancied himself quite the predator and developed that habit that housecats have of running out of the house between their human's legs when the biped arrives home at night. One day Jazz did not return, and a night or two later, I saw a *huge* barn owl – he must have been two feet tall – sitting on top of the house. I suddenly knew, with a sickening clarity, what had happened to poor, overconfident, Mr. Jazz.

I could have killed the owl, I suppose, but decided there was no reason. It was not as though he had killed for fun or sport like a human being would. He was only doing as God intended and I knew it was too late to save Mr. Jazz anyway. In fact, I was a little grateful that it was the owl and not coyotes that had gotten him. An owl hits its prey from behind at speeds up to 100 miles per hour, breaking their necks and killing them instantly. With coyotes, it is considerably more horrific and rarely instantaneous.

Enter Prescott.

Prescott

About three weeks after Mr. Jazz's death, a tiny, spotted kitten followed Fred home one afternoon when I let him out. I could still let Fred out because I knew that he never went out of sight of the house and that he never stayed out more than 15 minutes or so. His going out at night was no problem. He didn't do that because he was afraid of the dark.

The kitten, which I at first thought was a baby mountain lion, was as wild as a March Hare. As soon as he saw me, he made a beeline for a rat hole outside the back of the house. Luckily I got to him in time, and reaching into the hole, managed to grab his hindquarters before he either got stuck down there or met the rather large rodent – or whatever it was – that undoubtedly inhabited the place.

I dragged him out and brought both he and Fred into the house – for the last time. Neither has ever been outside since. I named him "Prescott" in honor of the late Mr. Jazz, and then wondered how Lazarus would react.

He wasn't particularly interested in the kitten, (which turned out to be half ocelot), at least at first. One day, I was in the kitchen doing the dishes when Laz strolled in – with the kitten in his mouth. More accurately, it was the kitten's HEAD that was in his mouth, with Prescott's little body hanging down in front of Laz's chest, all four legs sticking out like a little stick man. My heart all but stopped.

Laz was somewhat mystified by my subsequent behavior as I began leaping about the kitchen, shouting "NO, NO!! OUT!!" over and over again. Finally he dropped the kitten, apparently to give me his un-divided attention so that he could figure out just exactly what in the hell was wrong with me.

Prescott didn't run away. He hit the floor, stood there for a few moments, and then rubbed himself against Laz's foreleg. I was astounded. Had he actually ENJOYED the experience? The view, I knew, must have been extraordinarily unique, but still...

OF WARNINGS...

And that was what became Laz's pack for the rest of his life. The pecking order was me, Laz, Prescott, Blanche, and little Freddy was the Omega Man. Fred was always a bit wary of Laz – I couldn't blame him – and several times over the years, Laz would re-establish his dominance over the rest. This invariably scared the living hell out of whichever of the critters he was disciplining – and me. It was fascinating, though, in retrospect. On various occasions, all of them – Blanche, Prescott, and Fred, were in Laz's mighty maw, but believe it or not, not one of them was ever hurt.

Once, I stupidly let Blanche begin to lick from the other side of a plate that Laz was licking. I was sitting there, holding the plate, thinking how cute it was that they were "sharing" when Laz suddenly exploded in a blur of motion. I was *looking* at him and couldn't really follow what happened. All I knew was that he was suddenly on

Blanche, who was screaming and backing away, trying to defend herself. I couldn't even see her and he was making this ungodly terrible roaring sound that never failed to make my blood run cold. And, even more terrifying, he was advancing on her steadily.

Dropping the plate, I lunged forward and grabbed him by the back of his collar. It took all of my strength to pull him off of her and as I did so, the thought occurred to me "What if he turns around and doesn't stop?" But there was nothing I could do about that, except hope to God he wouldn't. And he didn't.

And then came the real shocker. I looked down at Blanche, expecting her to be a bloody mess, at the very least. Blanche didn't have a mark on her. She was virtually covered in saliva, but he had never bitten down.

...AND FACTS

It was around that time that I went to the library to do some reading about wolves. It was a revelation. Whoever thinks wolves are just wild dogs should think again. They only *look* like dogs.

These specs are all generalized of course, as I am certainly no expert, and I am also relying on memory. But I'm sure you can imagine the shock that came with the realization that I had had this unimaginably powerful killer sleeping, unrestrained, in the house with me for the past several months!

Get this: Wolves have predator's vision, which means that they see anything that moves, just like cats. They also have heat vision, which is to say that if you are alive – they can see you by your body temperature. So, if you were trying to hide, it had better be behind something like a large rock. Otherwise, the wolf would actually see your body "aura." Nowhere to run, nowhere to hide.

Then came the statistic that tended to get everyone's attention: A Pit Bull has a bite pressure of about five hundred pounds per square inch (nothing to sneeze at!). A wolf has a bite pressure of *fifteen hundred* pounds per square inch – enough to pulverize bones the size of baseball bats – and we don't have any that big!

This means that one serious bite would cripple you, as there is no way to fix bones crushed to powder. A full-blown attack would mean certain death to an unarmed human being.

"What have I brought into my home?" I remember thinking. "He's liable to kill poor little Blanche – to say nothing of the cats!" As usual, where Laz was concerned, I was wrong. Not only did he not kill Blanche, he became her savior.

BLANCHE AND THE COYOTES

One day in the early winter of 1997, I heard Blanche barking out back. Now, to this day, Blanche barks at virtually everything (including me) – she is a "yap dog." But when she barks *non-stop* – it means that she sees something. It was broad daylight, so I wasn't at all surprised to see Blanche about 70 feet from the house. What *did* get my attention was what she was barking at: two of the largest coyotes I've ever seen. The coyotes were about 15 feet from her at the edge of the brush. One of them was lying down, and the other, sitting. It was as if they were saying "Hey, get a little closer. You can trust us..."

I called Blanche and she came to me. Then I drew my .45 and deliberately put a bullet between them. (I know they are pests and can be dangerous, but a personal code forbids me from killing them except in the most dire of circumstances). As the bullet whistled between their heads, they slowly got up and *walked* off into the brush. Afraid, they most definitely were not.

Several days later they came back, and this time, they weren't fooling. Once again, it was about 11 a.m. when I heard Blanche shrieking. *this* time, it sounded as though something *had* her. I rushed to the back door, just in time to see Blanche come rocketing out from behind the barn. The same two coyotes – I recognized them because of their size – were just behind her, clearly intending to run her down. And they would have, too, if not for what happened next.

I called her to me, but Blanche kept right on going in the direction she had been – around the front of the house, where Laz was on his chain.

When we were just hanging around the house, as we were that day, I put Laz on a chain out front. This chain was attached to a spike driven three feet into the ground. Balled up, this chain was too heavy for me to lift. Laz barely knew it was there.

As Blanche and her pursuers disappeared from my view, I raced from the back door to the front door, picking up a pistol off the table as I did so. This entire trip took about four to six seconds. I opened the front door, and then just stood there, gaping in awe. There, at my feet, lay the two coyotes, both twitching, both dead.

He had snapped their necks as they came around the corner – in about the same amount of time that it takes you to read this sentence.

I looked from the dead coyotes to Laz, who was looking at me happily and wagging his tail. Then I looked at Blanche, who seemed *deliriously* happy. Her entire body was wagging.

I then realized that my next problem was going to be getting the bodies away from Laz, who clearly – and justifiably – felt that he should be able to keep them. But one of our "rules" had to do with not letting him get a taste of too much fresh blood, at least at one sitting. So, I managed to distract him while I tossed the bodies out of range of his chain. "Good thing he can't break that chain and get away" I remember thinking. Duh…. Wrong again…

One thing was certain, though. As far as Blanche was concerned, Laz was John Wayne, Arnold Schwarzeneggar and Rin-Tin-Tin all rolled into one. From that day on, she always deferred to him. If she was eating and he walked into the room, she stepped back so that he could help himself to the food. Of course, this was done partially out of respect and love, and partially out of the knowledge of what he could do to her should he so choose.

In the first year of her life, before she met me, Blanche had to fend for herself, and had become quite a proficient little hunter. In fact, I was once amazed to see her get a bird before it could get off the ground! She crept up to it on her belly until she was about six feet away. The bird could see her, but as it turned out, underestimated the little orange dog. When the bird tried to take to the air, she rushed at it and actually managed to leap up and catch it as it took off.

At this point, she began hunting birds, rodents, whatever she could find. She didn't eat them. She just brought them to Laz. Little Blanche was paying tribute.

In the end, he accepted her so much, and she became so comfortable with him, that she routinely treated him as though he were a low bridge. She walked around underneath him, and frequently, if she felt threatened by something, she simply stayed there.

Rat-Tails

On one occasion, she had found and killed a rather large rat that she had brought to him. Unlike the other kills she had brought him, Laz didn't immediately munch this one right down. He had other plans...

I had come out to chop some wood. While I was thus engaged.

Laz strolled over to me, the dead rat in his mouth, dangling by its tail. I looked at him and grinned – something he made me do often. "That *is* disgusting, you know" I commented. Than, I went back to chopping wood. However, as I did so, I could see out of the corner of my eye that Laz was still standing there, as though he was waiting for something.

As it turned out, he *was* waiting for something… me.

As soon as I turned back to him and he knew he had my attention, Laz flipped the rat into the air and then caught it in his mouth as it came down, head first. I was instantly treated to the sound of its bones crunching as it rapidly – in about three bites – went down his gullet. Only the tail hung out of his mouth, like a grotesquely disgusting limp cigarette.

I had this image in my head of him saying to Blanche, a few minutes earlier: "Watch this. *This* ought to gross him out!"

Jimbo

After my wife departed with the goal of becoming my ex-wife, I found myself in something of a financial bind. I wasn't making enough at the newspaper to pay the bills, pure and simple. Consequently, I advertised in the newspaper for a roommate. If you have never done this, you are wise. It was one of the dumbest things I ever did, and that is saying something!

The guy who answered my ad we shall call "Jimbo." At first, he seemed to be a good guy. He said all the right things during the interview.

Plus, he had a cat that he seemed to care for, which is something that I personally, feel can be rather telling about someone's personality. Frequently, but not always…

More significantly, Jimbo also possessed several horses, at least one of which I would be permitted to ride. And yes, I confess, that was what made my decision for me. And a bad decision it was, too…

He was down from Montana, and later I realized that he never received any mail from there, despite the fact he claimed to have lived there for years. If I had been more aware, this would have told me something, too.

As a taller-than-average guy, I have a great deal of experience dealing with shorter-than-average men, some of whom seem to have a great deal to prove. This, of course, is not necessarily always the case. I have two good friends – Craig and Leland – you know who you are – who are short, yes, but their self-confidence *more* than makes up for it. Whenever I talk to either of these guys, I feel I am looking into his eyes. It is not the physical height of a man that makes a difference – it is the man himself.

Unfortunately, in the case of Jimbo, he was a man with a great deal to prove, but who was quite adept at concealing his insecurities. He seemed like a good guy, as I said, and I saw no reason not to trust him. Laz felt otherwise. I would later find out that he was nothing more than a drifter and had a past that was nebulous at best.

The house in Bent was arranged so that you had to walk down a hall to get to the only bathroom. This hall was connected at one end by the kitchen and at the other, the living room.

I occasionally like to take long baths and read and whenever I did this, Laz would lie in the hallway immediately in front of the bathroom door, effectively stopping any traffic that might come down that hall. *Unless*, of course, you didn't mind stepping over him.

Jimbo later confessed that the one and only time that he contemplated stepping over the Big Guy, Laz looked at him in a way that told Jimbo, in no uncertain terms, that this maneuver would be unwise in the extreme.

It wasn't until later that I put it together that Laz had been suspicious of this guy all along. And with good reason. One night I came home and Jimbo drunkenly confronted me, telling me that he was now the "boss" and that I would be doing what *he* said from now on. (This was *my* house, remember?)

Firstly, I had never considered myself the "boss," and secondly, I couldn't help but notice that Jimbo waited until Laz was outside before he got brave. He had lived there long enough to know that early arthritis prevents me from even making a fist. It would have been a pretty one-sided fight – which is always what appeals to bullies, come to think of it.

I kept a firearm handy from that day until this overgrown child moved out a few days later – at my request, of course. I have never seen him again, which is a good thing.

THE CHAIN

One morning in the spring of 1997, I awoke to hear the sound of Laz howling – he had not yet learned to bark – in the distance! I leaped out of bed and dressed as quickly as I could. Rushing outside, I found that the 3-foot spike, the heavy chain, and Laz were all gone. The howling was coming from somewhere up in the mountains. I began following the sound, but quickly realized that was unnecessary as there was a half-inch-deep furrow in the ground where he had dragged the chain.

About a quarter mile up in the mountains I found him where he had wrapped himself around a tree. He was happy to see me and I realized, a little late as usual, that I had a problem. I couldn't ball up this chain and carry it, as it was far too heavy, nor could I lead him down with it, thanks to all the obstructions strewn across the forest floor – dead trees and such – on that part of the mountain. All I could do was set him free, and drag the chain back down myself. There was a chance, or so I thought, of him running away.

But he went straight back to the house – it was, after all, where his pack lived.

Barking

Lazarus did not bark until he was nearly a year old. And then, it appeared he had to learn it from Blanche, who barked far *too* much.

I remember sitting in my living room watching him stroll up next to her as she barked – maniacally and ferociously, (well, as ferociously as possible for Blanche), at some unseen, and probably non-existent, enemy in the brush. God only knows what she saw or thought she saw, but whatever it was had long since departed, if it had ever been there in the first place.

Laz stared into the brush intently for a minute or so. Then he looked down at Blanche, who had never stopped barking. Then he looked back into the brush. Finally he sat down, alternately looking from Blanche to the brush and back again. Clearly, he was mystified by the strange behavior being exhibited by his new friend, the tiny, orange wolf.

A few days later, Blanche was at it again, but this time there was a roadrunner bouncing around in the low branches of a tree. *this*, Laz could see. He puffed out his chest and... well, it's hard to describe. What passed for a bark with Laz was sort of a high-volume, abbreviated growl. The word "baritone" does not begin to describe the depth of the sound.

Of course, howling was much more up his alley. Occasionally, just to be silly, I would begin howling in the house. Laz would look intensely at me, get agitated, and then join in and we would have ourselves a little hootenanny. Sometimes, I would even play my electric guitar and he would sing along with that. He seemed to like the key of B flat...

When he was outside, alone, and wanted to come in, he would usually bark once. However, if I didn't hear him, he would then proceed to howl. It was the saddest sound I could ever have imagined, and invariably had me rushing for the back door. I just couldn't take the terrible despair that the sound of his lonely howl seemed to possess. He had my behavior as fine-tuned as a Swiss watch.

In the fall of 1997, I accepted a job in Lincoln, New Mexico as a historian. The scene of the Lincoln County War and Billy the Kid's rise to legendary status is a dream place for *any* western historian to work. The problem was that I lived 70 miles away in Bent, and it took me an hour and a half one way to get to work, which in turn, aggravated my sciatica – my bad back. The situation finally became intolerable, and I found a nice little place in Lincoln to live – a two-bedroom house was plenty for me, but as always, I had to make special arrangements for the critters – especially you-know-who.

Now, with work only a mile away, things became a lot easier. I decided to have a compound built, primarily for Laz, with some of the money I received from the sale of the house in Bent. The way it worked, I could just open the back door and Laz (as well as Blanche, of course) could step outside into a fenced area that kind of wound around my pump house, chicken coop and storage building (and no, I didn't keep chickens – much as Laz would have liked it). It wasn't as big as I would have liked either, but the Big Guy seemed happy with it.

Occasionally, after its completion, I would inadvertently leave one of the two gates open and go outside to find the gate swinging and Laz gone. I would have a more or less instantaneous nervous breakdown, but would inevitably find him poking around, sniffing curiously around the house.

While the compound was being built, I kept him, once again, on that spike in the ground, on the chain. You can imagine how often I checked on him after my last experience with that chain. I would leap into my car and zoom home every hour or so, only to find Laz looking curiously at me as I turned around and headed back to work.

Laz was fully grown by this time. Standing 33 inches at the shoulder and weighing in at 160 lbs., he was an impressive – a magnificent – figure.

THE HORSE AND THE GOAT

While I had lived in Bent, I had rented out some pasture space to a person who kept about nine horses there. One of them was an elderly, grey thoroughbred named "Chance." He seemed to be the ramuda's pariah, ostracized by the others (there's always one), and I felt sorry for him. Also, his health wasn't that good, and I didn't feel that his owner did enough for him. When I moved to Lincoln, I simply asked if I could take him with me. As I had suspected, she was glad to get him off her hands. I have never been of the opinion that once a horse is old and useless it should go to the glue factory. I feel that as they work for us all their lives, they are entitled to retirement, too.

The problem was that, despite the fact that Chance had been the "odd man out" among the other horses – they were still the only horses he had for company. Being taken away from them was terribly traumatic for him. Horses are herd animals, they *need* other horses.

It was torture for me to watch this lonely old horse poke around in the pasture, yearning for company. He would become *so* happy when I went out and kept him company that it finally made me ashamed. Happily, a solution was forthcoming – in the form of a baby goat.

Some friends up the road had just had a goat "blessed event" and now had two kids that they needed to find homes for – I don't know if you have ever been around a baby goat, but no animal is more playful, entertaining – or mischievous. He was a few-months-old South African Boar goat who was all white with a brown head. I named him "Ed."

Horses and goats get on notoriously well, and Ed and Chance were no exception.

Chance only lived another year, but it was most gratifying to see that now-happy, elderly horse cavorting and bounding around the pasture like a colt, with his tiny friend.

Chance doted on Ed. If Chance were to lie down on his side, Ed would climb up on him for a nap. When Chance wanted to get up, he would – ever so gently – shake the little fellow off. He even groomed him. They were happy with each other in their little world.

THE BATTLE OF THE PASTURE

Drought conditions had been horrendous that year, and many predators were coming down out of the mountains in search of food. At the time, I was working on fencing the pasture with goat fencing in addition to the barbed wire that was already there, but had not quite finished. There was no problem about Ed leaving – he was determined to stay with Chance. It was what might get INTO the pasture from the outside that worried me.

One night, about three in the morning, Blanche and Laz began barking outside in the compound, and the urgent sound of it virtually catapulted me out of bed. Both of them were looking toward the pasture. Laz was snarling. When I looked out there, (there was no moon) I could make out Chance's huge grey frame bucking and kicking and there seemed to be a small white spot directly underneath him, which I realized was Ed. This seemed to be a bad place for the little guy to be until I noticed that, all around, there were other, more shadowy figures, moving quickly and stealthily about. Chance was the only one making any noise. The coyote pack was silent, determined... and deadly.

Before racing for a rifle, I opened the door and let Laz, who had followed me back into the house from the compound, out. As I grabbed the weapon and exited the house myself, the sound of the battle in the pasture began to change. The coyotes were screaming.

As I said, I had partially fenced the pasture (with five-foot high fencing) and the result was that I had to run to the far end of it to go through the gate. As I did, a coyote almost ran between my legs in his desperate zeal to get away from what was happening behind him. I'm not sure he even noticed me.

It was all over by the time I got there. Despite the fact that the few surviving coyotes were gone, poor terrified (but unhurt) little Eddie had elected to stay underneath Chance for a while. His gaze was riveted on Laz, who had a dead coyote in his mouth. Altogether, there were three dead. Laz definitely killed two of them, but Chance may have gotten one, too. At any rate, he sure must have stepped on it, as it was pretty flat. Again, I had to get the bodies away from Laz and then get Laz away from Ed before the Big Guy got any ideas about perhaps making a clean sweep of any animals smaller than himself in the entire pasture.

Of Psychics and Rodents

Life with Lazarus was always interesting and never dull. As time passed, I found that I could play quite roughly with him – and live to tell the tale. I could cuff him about, and he would play-growl and grab me with his teeth, *all* of which were on display. If someone did not understand the nature of our relationship, it tended to look as though he was about to kill me.

What most people never realized, because they never heard the real thing, was that it was quite easy to tell Laz's play-growl from the genuine sound. His real growl was easily identified because it made the hair on the back of one's neck stand on end.

After the battle in the pasture, Laz's only victims were the occasional rodents who inadvisedly wandered into his compound. One day, I found Blanche attacking a fairly large rat, which had come up from a nearby cistern. She would dart in, snap, and dart back again. The more she did this, the more disoriented the injured rat became. Finally, both Blanche and I watched in dumbfounded amazement (Blanche even sat down and stared) as the rat wobbled and stumbled toward the compound, where Laz had been seated, silently watching.

I looked at Blanche as the rat began to unsteadily make his way under the gate. Blanche looked back at me. I said aloud, "I dunno. Suicidal, I guess." At just that moment, the rat cleared the fence and was dead in a second. Maybe he really *was* going for a quick death. It certainly was faster than Blanche's method.

It was around this time that a friend of mine, who wishes to remain anonymous, came to visit. The reason this lady prefers anonymity is the fact that she is a genuine psychic. Yes, I was skeptical, too. But when she began telling me things about my pets, at first marveling at how much they loved me, and then telling me certain things that she could not have known otherwise, I gradually became convinced.

She commented that she wished that her animals loved her as much as mine did me, which was, of course, terribly flattering. Some of the stuff she told me was no surprise. For instance, she informed me that Blanche's routine was "very important to her." This made perfect sense, as dogs like routine and the first year or so of Blanche's life had been sadly lacking in any kind of structure.

But it was what she told me about Laz that got my attention.

She told me that he *knew* that he could kill me any time he wanted. He *deliberately* suppressed his natural predator's instincts out of love for me.

And that, my friends, is the greatest gift I have ever received. Wolves aren't supposed to love anyone but other wolves, yet this massive, magnificent, unimaginably dangerous character loved me. Never, before or since, have I been so deeply flattered or felt so blessed.

CHANCE DEPARTS

In May of 1999, two days before my 50th birthday, Chance died. As always, such a thing was traumatic for me, as I know it is for most animal owners who care for their charges. The old guy had had cancer for some time, and it was getting to the point where he was in pain – and I couldn't allow that.

That day, the vet came over and gave Chance "the shot." I was so distraught, I didn't even think about poor Ed, who was now fully grown. He had stood there in the pasture and watched his life-long friend collapse, die, and then be buried. Ed began to howl, if that is even the word for the sounds he began making. Perhaps "wailing" is a better word. Whatever word you use, the little guy was grieving.

There was no keeping Eddie in the pasture after that, either. Like horses, goats are herd animals and hate to be alone. They are also escape artists when they want to be. Ed would carry on terribly before inevitably winding up at one of my living room windows, peering in, undoubtedly wondering why he, and he alone, was not allowed inside. Luckily, Ed's mother had just given birth again and had triplets (Sadly, goats usually only have 2 babies, and this was too much for her. The birth killed her).

I requested one of the kids, who was actually Ed's full brother (same father, too) and named him Steve. Like his brother Ed, Steve had a white body, but unlike Ed, his head was white, with streaks and different shades of browns, with white streaks.

Finally, it appeared that Ed was placated, although I would occasionally notice that he seemed to stare intently at Chance's grave.

In 2000, I began to feel guilty that Lazarus had such a small world. Eventually, I elected to load him into the car at least once a weekend, and take him into town. He loved this. I would parade him up the street, and he gloried in all the smells and sights. I guess it was sort of like Disneyworld for him. And I have to admit, the fact that he was so special made me feel special, too.

I don't think he was ever lonely. Dianne Stallings – "grandma," if you will, came by to visit him on a regular basis. For most of his life, when he saw someone he cared for, he would first, stand on his hind legs, and then leap straight up into the air. This made his head reach a height of about seven feet. It was spectacular to watch, too. Unfortunately, it was very bad for his spine, and he eventually slipped a disc. I *did* manage to get a photo of him doing it, though. One thing that I am extremely glad about, now that he is gone, is that I did take so many photos – including a professionally-made video – with which to remember him.

After his death, I also learned how popular he really was with other people, but that was not for another four years. I had always loved him. It never even occurred to me that he had something of a local fan club. People liked to be able to tell their friends how they had petted a wolf – and a huge one at that.

Of course Laz had Blanche, who loved and revered him. And there were the cats, but I'm not sure Laz, or for that matter, the cats themselves, were ever completely convinced that they weren't horsd'oeuvres.

One wintry day, I took him out in the snow. He and Steve actually touched noses through the fence, with Steve inclining his head in the classic goat "Hey, how do ya' do? Lemme butt ya!" greeting. Frankly, I was extremely apprehensive and glad that the fence was there. I kept a close eye on Laz, who seemed only curious, not aggressive.

As time went by I learned more and more from Laz. Over the years, we established so many unspoken rules that it was though we had our own constitution – kind of like the U.S. Constitution, actually, with amendments being added regularly.

There were certain things he did and didn't do, and certain things I did and didn't do. He didn't try to take food off my plate – as long as I was there, anyway. If I wasn't present, he figured all bets were off.

I used to tell guests that if they had some broach or other small object that meant a lot to them, to be sure and keep it secured in their suitcase, or some other place where Laz would not go. Because, you see, once it was in his mouth, as far as both he *and* I were concerned, it was *his*.

Much of our communication had to do with him grabbing me with his teeth. If he wanted to tell me something, or was simply showing exuberant affection, he would suddenly – and faster than the human eye could follow – grasp my forearm. With most of my lower arm inside his mouth, he never, ever, so much as scratched me, although his grip was certainly firm enough. And I can also attest to the fact that it tends to get one's attention rather dramatically.

He never chewed anything up, either, and when you think about *that*, it's a fairly amazing fact in itself. Lazarus' first chew-toys in Lincoln were some railroad ties that I had brought in to line the bottom of his compound in case he decided to dig his way out. (He never did.) What he did do was re-arrange these railroad ties on a regular basis – as though they were tinker toys.

However, and as previously stated, if he should pick something up with those teeth of his, be it a family heirloom or whatever, you could kiss it goodbye. Once it was in his toothsome maw, well, those half-inch fangs would deter all but the most foolhardy.

They sure as hell deterred *me*.

"CHUCK"

A good illustration of the inadvisability of attempting to remove something – anything – from Laz's mouth was an encounter with a friend of mine we shall call Chuck.

Chuck was a good guy – he has since passed on – but he was kind of short, and like many men of small physical (key word) stature, he had something of a yen to prove himself.

One evening in 1999, Chuck dropped over the house to visit. He had been drinking quite a bit, which has some bearing on what happened that night. I was seated in an easy chair and Chuck sat across from me on the couch. In front of the couch was a long, low table. Between that table and the couch lay Lazarus, happily munching down a paper towel.

When Laz was a baby, Dianne had given him the cores to toilet paper rolls as toys, and his puppy-like enthusiasm for paper products carried over into his adult life. Every time I would use a paper towel as a napkin – and sometimes *before* I got the opportunity, he would snatch it, tear it into pieces and eat it. He digested all this just fine, so I never had any problem with him doing it.

Anyway, Chuck looked down and saw that Laz was chewing on something. "Uh-oh," he said, "he's got something." And with that, he began to reach down toward Laz's head. I immediately interjected that Laz didn't even let *me* take anything out of his mouth, and that he should just be left alone.

What I should have said was that I had given the paper towel to Laz to play with in the first place, but for some reason, I didn't. Consequently, my confessing that I was unable to accomplish the task of removing something from the Big Guy's mouth, was to Chuck, a challenge. Chuck's hand kept snaking down. "I think I can get it," he reiterated several more times. I, in turn, just kept repeating, "No Chuck, no…" but Chuck wasn't to be denied.

Finally Laz lifted his head slightly, and let out a low guttural sound that wasn't quite a growl. For me, though, it had the unmistakable sound of a warning. *Still*, Chuck's hand advanced. Suddenly there was a gray blur – a short roar – and it was over.

Chuck had immediately jerked his hand away and held it over his head. Laz instantly went back to working on the paper towel. "Damn, that was close," said Chuck, "he almost got me."

It was then that I noticed the blood running down his arm. Laz had given him a little warning nip that consisted of only one fang puncturing the palm of his hand. It did not go all the way through, although it seemed close. Once again, I was actually watching, but the action was too fast for my eyes to follow. And Chuck had to be *told* it had happened.

To Chuck's great credit, he then said, "You know Drew, that was one of the dumbest things I've ever done. He could have killed me." And he could have, too. But he never really wanted to hurt anyone – he just didn't want to me messed with. Who does?

PEDICURES

Warren Franklin is my vet and he is a good one. On numerous occasions, he literally stuck his head – or at least his hand – into the "lion's mouth," so to speak. In fact, he *had* to do this about twice a year. That was because it was about twice a year that I had to have Laz's nails trimmed. It was a chore I dreaded, and I'm sure the Doc did, too.

What was kind of funny was because of the turnover in Doc's office for a few years, no two people ever had to deal with Laz more than once, which, after having done it once, was undoubtedly a relief for them.

Inevitably, anyone unfamiliar with Laz would make some remark to the effect that "Hey, what's the big deal? It's just trimming a dog's nails, right?" Remarks like this would, without exception, sent me, and occasionally the Doc, into paroxysms of laughter.

The only way for them to truly understand the overall *excitement* of trimming Laz's nails was to actually do it. This involved first, wrapping surgical gauze around his muzzle and tying it behind his head. Then, at least two of us, preferably three, would lie on top of him after forcing him to the ground, no easy feat in itself. Then, the Doc would go around from paw to paw, alternately trimming Laz's nails and leaping backwards when Laz would suddenly jerk his head around. It was extremely tough to hold him down. I can't even begin to describe his strength, especially after he reached his peak weight of 160 lbs.

That surgical gauze stretches, too, so no matter how tightly we tied it, he managed to loosen it about a quarter inch – just enough to get a little taste of whomever he could reach… In between lunges, he howled…

I always lay on his shoulders and neck. I figured if *somebody* had to be bit, it should be me. But it was never me he *wanted* to bite. He was forever trying to push past me to get at one of the others. "*Drew*," he seemed to say, "at least let me nail *one* of them!"

Eventually, the Doc's clinic just made sure that they had a full crew on duty the day Laz came for his pedicure. One of my great, and as it turned out, unfounded, fears was that Laz would become ill for some time and would require a good deal of medical attention – something he was obviously loathe to receive.

In 2003, I began to do some television work for the History Channel. This involved me flying regularly to Hollywood to film. Occasionally, I would have to stay as long as a week and I worried constantly. Various friends in Lincoln volunteered to take care of Laz and the other critters, because they knew how much I cared for them.

Invariably, I would call about once a day to find out if all was well. No matter who the sitter was, I was always told the same thing: "Everything's fine. The animals are all OK. Enjoy yourself." This was a nice, thoughtful, intentionally re-assuring message, so I never did get around to pointing out that I wasn't worried so much about the animals as the sitters!

Lazarus never went after anyone without a reason. The problem was, anyone used to dealing with dogs was likely to inadvertently give him a reason. Laz was no dog, and that was what everyone had a problem with. I was forever receiving instructions on how to "train" him. Hah.

Now, in point of fact, I do actually know how to train dogs. The problem was, Laz *was no dog*. If you tried to take something out of his mouth, you could get your arm ripped off. If you were insane enough to take a rolled-up newspaper, or anything else that looked like a weapon to him, you could actually get killed.

Besides, you can't train a wild animal. Every time I would get his attention, it would be diverted by say, a butterfly – thanks to his predator's vision. In the end, and many people have a problem understanding this too, you *cannot* domesticate a wild animal. Period. So don't ask if the person with the wild animal has been able to "domesticate" him. Domestic animals are born, not made.

It is also interesting to note that wolves have not evolved in 20,000 years, for the simple reason that there is no further need. They are perfect predators. Everything about them compliments everything else. Their front paws, for example, are splayed for digging, and anyone who has ever seen one dig a hole three feet deep in about a minute, knows of which I speak.

Laz also had the classic wild animal double coat. No matter how hard I tried, I never seemed able to get down to his skin. In the snow, he would walk into the house, covered in snow, shake off, and be instantly dry. It took poor little Blanche hours of lying in front of the fire to dry off.

A wolf's eyes are set in it's head differently than a dog's, too.

A wolf can still scan the horizon with his nose to the ground. A dog cannot. The list of differences goes on and on. In the end, the inescapable conclusion is that these animals, while they may look like dogs, are something else. Something else entirely. Something far more dangerous, far more mysterious, and something that Man is still attempting, mostly without success, to understand.

Someone once commented to me that it would not be fair to pit an average dog against an average wolf in a fight. He said that, in a combat situation, the dog would not be in the wolf's league.

Now, *that* is understatement. Not in it's league? It's not even the same sport!

THE GOUGE

In the winter of 2003, some relatives of a friend of mine asked to be able to come and meet Laz. They arrived, about four adults, and a whopping six kids. Now, Laz had never been one for crowds, and my living room is not that big, so I should have seen this coming. But I didn't. As usual, I was far too complacent.

Whenever strangers would meet him, I would give them a little speech about how to behave. "Never, never" I would tell them, "do you want to lock eyes with him." To Laz, that was a challenge. Unfortunately, this usually had the effect of people petting him with their eyes riveted on the ceiling. Seems no one could quite get straight the difference between looking into his eyes and staring into them.

That was OK, though, I figured. Better to be safe than sorry. But this time, it just didn't work out. In retrospect, I strongly suspect that the young lady in question provoked Laz.

After my "Don't stare into his eyes" speech, I had all of them go to the far end of the room. They wanted pictures with him and I knew he didn't like to be crowded, so I told them "one at a time." I got him to sit, which luckily, he felt like doing, and then I crouched next to him, looping my right hand through the back of his collar and placing my left arm across his chest. I had him under control, or so I thought.

The problem was, one of the kids, a girl of about 12, *also* thought I had him. And, kids being kids, she decided that this was a good time to test out that "staring" thing I had told her about. (If I'm wrong about this, I apologize to the young lady, but I don't think I am, because it was only her in whom he was interested, as he actually pushed past others to get to her).

Well, she locked eyes with him and I felt a low rumble in his chest vibrating into my arm and escalating in volume. Then he went for her. I still "had" him, and consequently was dragged along like so much baggage. He simply took me with him… like I wasn't even there. Laz pushed past the other people and, making that terrible roaring sound, struck.

Once again, thank God, it was a warning. The little girl had about a five-inch groove in her forearm that had barely drawn blood. It sure as hell got her attention, though. The poor kid was hysterical for quite some time, but I was informed later that, by the end of the day, she was proudly displaying her "wolf scar." (Even now, I would like to extend my thanks to her folks for not suing me!).

That was the last time Laz was allowed around children. It wasn't him I distrusted. It was the kids.

THE FIBER FEST

Every year Lincoln, where I make my home, hosted something called the "Fiber Fest." Personally, I'm not much for attending events of any sort and had never actually been to a Fiber Fest. In the summer of 2002, when I was taking Laz for his weekly walk through town (I must confess, he really did literally stop traffic and I enjoyed it), I saw that the yearly festival was in progress and elected to walk over and find out exactly what it was. Of course, as the name implies, it was all about fibers – wool, etc.

Unfortunately, as Laz and I rounded a corner of the pageant grounds in Lincoln where the event is held, we suddenly found ourselves looking at a small, temporary corral that was set up by a gentleman who had brought some live sheep. There were five of them in the corral, and they reacted – well, DRAMATICALLY to say the least, when Lazarus and I hove into view.

I was unaware of this, but apparently sheep have several defense mechanisms. Defense mechanisms is probably a misnomer, but in any case… I am told that when a sheep is attacked, it's body releases powerful endorphins so that they don't feel much, if any pain. How true that particular fact is I don't know, but seeing is believing…

Of course, he didn't attack them – I had a pretty good grip on his leash at all times – but those sheep looked at Laz and he looked at them, and three of them promptly fainted. The owner, seeing this, immediately began imploring me to take Laz away "before they have heart attacks." I thought he was joking, but have since been told that a sheep-coronary would have been a real possibility. The two who didn't faint busied themselves using the bodies of their fallen comrades to try and climb out of the corral and escape this monster who had suddenly appeared. I guess it is safe to say that Lazarus definitely ruined their day, and I'm quite certain, from the intense interest he was showing, that given the opportunity, he really would have dined on them. After all, that was who he was.

THE COOKIE

By the beginning of 2004, I noticed that Laz no longer did his leap-into-the-air-on-his-hind-legs trick when I got home at night. He was slowing down. Nevertheless, every now and then, he would remind me of his considerable abilities – just in case I had forgotten.

One night, there was no moon and it was black as pitch outside. Inside, it was even worse by the back door, where there was no real window. I actually had to grope my way to the door (I do this sort of thing often. It is a rare occasion indeed that I actually remember to replace a light bulb until a month or two after it has burned out). Finally, I reached down and felt for the door latch. Finding it, I lifted it to let Laz and Blanche in.

I heard Blanche scurry past me in the darkness and at the same time realized that I had a cookie in my other hand. Instinctively, I simply held the hand with the cookie in it above my head – away from Laz – or so I thought.

Now, I am about 6'2" and wear high-heeled cowboy boots. I was holding this cookie a few inches above my head when I felt the soft fur on Laz's upper lip brush my fingers and voila! The cookie was gone. Those teeth, a fraction of an inch away, had never touched me. He used them like precision instruments. All I could do was shake my head and smile. It had been my last cookie, too.

In my research about wolves, I had learned that, in the wild, they can live up to 14 years. But I had not taken into account the dog blood in Laz's veins. Negligible as it was, it still made him a hybrid, and hybrids, I found out too late, rarely live more than eight years.

THE REUNION

In October of 2002, I held a reunion (of sorts) for my buddies from my service time overseas (1968-72) at my house in Lincoln. I say "of sorts" because, essentially, I just contacted everyone, let them know how to get to my house and announced that, other than putting a roof over their heads, I wasn't going to do anything that resembled work.

As I said, they are my buddies from the military, and if anyone knows me, it is they, so no one was surprised at this announcement. I *did* make a point of making sure that everyone understood that they would be sleeping in the same house that contained an enormous – and unrestrained – wolf.

Larry "Bobo" Wilson, John Middleton, Craig Roche, Paul Black, Mike Manning, and Larry Benanti were the old friends who came, and there is not one of them in whose hands I would not place my life without a second thought, and I think that explains why Laz made them more welcome than he had ever made anyone, before or since, with the possible exceptions of my mother and sister – and, of course, Dianne Stallings. But Dianne didn't really count – she was family.

I only had enough room to put up a few of the guys overnight, but all six of them were at the house most of the time. I was a tad concerned, although I didn't say anything to the guys, about Laz.

For Laz, this was an enormous crowd to have in the house. So of course, he did the strangest thing – something I didn't, but probably should have expected. I guess he sensed the bonds that existed between these guys and myself, as I mentioned above. Not only were there no problems, I noticed that he greeted each one of them individually as though each one were an old friend.

One night we had a cookout out back, about 40 feet beyond Laz's compound. One of the guys, Larry Benanti, was going back and forth from the house with various utensils and – most significantly to Laz – meat. As Larry drew abreast of Laz's compound, the Big Guy would silently pace along next to him – Laz's unspoken food lust apparent in the extreme. As Larry stated later, "If he had wanted to come and get it, I would have been *happy* to give it to him!"

The only near-incident that occurred was when Craig Roche was sitting on the couch in the living room. We were all there and Laz lumbered over and climbed up onto the couch next to Craig. I grabbed my camera for the "Kodak moment" that it was, but as I took the picture, I noticed a couple of things. One was that Craig was eating a piece of jerky. Another was that Laz *knew* Craig was eating a piece of jerky. And still another was that it was apparent to me, if no one else, that Laz was about to *take* that hunk of meat out of Craig's hand – whether Craig liked it or not. I knew Laz well enough to know that unless Craig remained absolutely motionless, he could be in serious trouble.

Towering over Craig, Laz's body language told me that he was about to move. Dropping the camera, I lunged forward and grabbed him by the collar, pulling him off the couch and away from Craig (at least until Craig was finished with that damn jerky).

When the photo was developed, it told the story. I could see, thanks to this photograph, that I had not been mistaken. In the picture, Craig and Laz are looking right at each other, with Laz looking *down* on Craig. At a glance it is a humorous photo. But to me, it was an ominous reminder. Sweet as he was to my friends, Laz would always be a wolf and it is an extremely bad idea to introduce food into a social mix like the one that existed that day. In the wild, food is considered to be worth both dying and killing for.

To this day, the photo sits, framed, in my living room. I put it there as a reminder to try and *never* forget who Laz was, and to never again become complacent with him. And you know what? That *never worked*!!

It is very difficult to be wary of a creature who never shows you anything but love. It seemed that, as time passed, I always managed to get complacent with Laz, and he would, sooner or later, have to remind me of exactly who I was dealing with.

THE END OF THE TRAIL

In January of 2004, I was in the compound with him, playing tug-of-war with a large, heavy rubber "indestructible" ball that I had gotten him as a toy. These things are actually made for horses, and I guess maybe if a horse had it – or a regular dog – it *would* have been indestructible.

It was indestructible for about 30 seconds after Laz got hold of it, and had been flat for some time the day we were playing with it.

I could see that he was getting *very* excited by the wild look on his face. Suddenly, when I let go of the ball, he let go of it, too… It dropped, forgotten, between us. Those killers' eyes, for the very first time, bored into mine and I knew that if I moved a muscle, I would be prey. I had crossed the line. I had gotten him *far* too excited.

The only thing on me that moved was my mouth.

Keeping my tones calm and low, I began speaking to him, gently imploring him to calm down. As per usual, he was ahead of me. I could actually see the aggression go out of his eyes as he turned and loped over to the back door, where he stood, wagging his tail and waiting to be let in. It was as if he was saying "Best go inside now, Drew. This has gone a little too far." He was right. We went inside and took a nap.

Lazarus had never been sick a day in his life. In August of 2004, I was summoned, once again, to Hollywood for a week or so to do some filming. As I had in the recent past, I called upon my friend and neighbor, Cille Dickinson, to come and take care of my critters.

I will be forever grateful to Cille for not calling me in Los Angeles when Laz began to become ill. There was nothing I could have done, other than give myself an ulcer from worrying. When I did get home, late on the night of the 26th, I noticed that he didn't get right up when I came in, and seemed sort of lethargic. I immediately called Cille, who told me that she had not been able to get him up and had called the vet. She also was concerned over whether or not she had done the right thing. She had, and as I said, I will always be grateful.

I spent the weekend trying to get Laz to eat, but to no avail. He would have none of it. On Monday, deeply concerned, I finally took him to the vet. He stayed at the Franklin Veterinary Clinic overnight and the next day, the prognosis sounded pretty good. They had managed to get some meds into him and he had eaten. At this point, before the blood work came back, it was thought that he had heatstroke.

However, when I took him home, he immediately went back to lying in the living room, acting weak and tired, and not eating. More importantly, he wanted no part of the medication.

This was what I had dreaded for so long. To attempt to make Laz do something he didn't want to could have catastrophic results – which was something I knew from experience. I decided to get brave and attempt, at least, to "pill" him the way one would a regular dog. This is accomplished by bringing the hand down over the top of the muzzle, using the thumb and middle finger to push the animal's upper lip into his fangs, which then causes him to open his mouth. Once the mouth is open, the pill is inserted as far as possible down the throat. The mouth is closed and held shut and with your other hand, you rub the dog's throat to produce a swallowing reflex.

This is easy enough with dogs, but a wolf? Laz had never in his life tolerated being handled in such a fashion – by anyone, even me. Therefore, it was with the greatest trepidation when I cautiously reached over to open his mighty maw. Much to my amazement, he allowed me to do it. Unfortunately, he didn't swallow the pill and immediately spit it out when I released him. However, I was encouraged, so I tried it again. Again, he spit the pill out. The third time, when I went to reach for him, he curled his lip, ever so slightly. If it had been someone else, the gesture might have been too subtle to notice, but Laz and I had known each other too long for the message not to be clear: "That's enough. You've already gotten away with a lot."

And I had, too. Had any other living creature attempted to do what I did, he or she would have paid a terrible price in blood. Even sick, Laz was dangerous and strong. But because of his great capacity for love, he permitted me to "handle" him – that which he hated above all else. As always, I was deeply flattered.

But now, things were beginning to become clear. Lazarus knew something I didn't. He wanted no more food, and he certainly wanted no meds. I believe he felt that his time had come.

We spent the next several days just lying around the house – literally. One night, I slept next to him on the floor. I took a number of pictures, even though I certainly had a large supply taken over the years, including a video we made on New Year's Day of 2003. Still, I couldn't bring myself to stop.

The vet had finally gotten the blood work back and the prognosis was bad. It hadn't been heatstroke. It was renal failure. His liver and kidneys were giving out.

The only alternative to me giving him meds at home was to take him and leave him at the vet's. The one night he had spent there a few days previous had been the first night he had ever spent away from home. I didn't want to subject him to that stress again, and when the Doc told me that he could possibly die at the clinic anyway, I knew what I had to do.

Laz was right. His time really *had* come. As always, he was the teacher and I was the student – so much for "training" him, right? He had known all along. I began to notice that when he was awake, he tended to focus on one of two things, either he would stare at the mountains, or he would stare at me.

My heart is still breaking as I write this. The Doc had told me that Laz would be comfortable until he began throwing up and developing sores on his gums. Wednesday night, the 1st of September, he vomited twice. I called the vet the first thing in the morning. He said he would be over directly.

I hung up the phone and looked down at my friend, my brother. His tail wagged weakly. I lay down on the floor with him, and we were together for an hour or so until the Doc got there. I tried to be cheery to hopefully, put him at ease. As always, he was way ahead of me.

The Doc and his assistant, Sara, pulled in about 11:30 on the morning of the 2nd of September. The Doc told me to take my time, that he was in "no hurry." When he looked at my friend, he also said, "I don't even know if I can do this." The Doc had treated Laz all of his life, initially listing him, just for the sake of the record, as a "Husky." As I stated earlier, he is a good man.

I brought Laz outside for the final time. We walked together around the property, which is only about an acre and a half. He had to rest twice, but when we got to the pasture, Steve, the younger goat, strolled over. I watched as he and Laz touched noses through the fence.

Perhaps it's me, but I believe Laz was saying goodbye. Ed, on the other hand, never would get within 20 feet of the Big Guy. Ed remembered what Laz had done to those coyotes, and was not about to take any chances. He stood in the middle of the pasture and watched as Laz and I strolled back toward the house.

Blanche had been sitting, silently watching, from the compound. As we drew abreast of her, she walked next to us, on her side of the fence, whimpering. Laz stopped one last time to touch noses with his life-long friend. Then, like a courageous condemned man, he walked to the front of the house and sat down on the tarpaulin that I had laid there.

The Doc explained how it worked. Laz would be given a powerful anesthetic and after he was asleep, the euthanasia would be administered in IV form, and brain activity would shut down. He said he had made the anesthetic shot strong, because, after treating Laz for the last nine years, he knew that even in a weakened condition, Lazarus was a force with which to be reckoned.

The Doc administered the shot and we waited. And waited. And waited. Again, I noticed that Laz's gaze continually alternated between me and the mountains.

Finally, I asked the Doc exactly how strong the shot had been. He shook his head and said "Enough for a large horse." For the first time that day, it brought a smile to my lips. Ornery to the last, I remember thinking... After the second shot, the Doc picked up Laz's leg, knowing the Big Guy's life-long aversion to being handled, expecting him not to react, proving that he was asleep. Immediately, Laz's lip curled...

In the end, it took enough anesthetic for 2 and a half large horses to put him into dreamland. Then, they put in the needle and his great heart, so full of love, affection, and millenniums of wisdom, finally stopped beating. Just for a moment, I wished mine would, too. My friend, my son, my brother, was gone.

I was once in a saloon where someone had carved into the bar "Father Sun, Mother Moon, Brother Wolf." They sure had that right. Those are the words I put on Laz's marker.

I deal best with grief in a solitary fashion, and consequently had not asked anyone except my friend Ira Rabke, who had cared for Laz on many an occasion when I was out of town, to come over and help me get my friend to his grave. I knew that it was going to be a tough and grim job. The previous day, I had a friend dig a deep trench with a backhoe. Ira arrived and a few minutes later, so did Cille Dickinson. She got out of her truck and said, "I know you asked me not to come over, Drew, but I had to say goodbye."

It made me realize how selfish I had been. I hadn't been the only one who loved him, although I truly believe that, much as he liked other people, Dianne Stallings (grandma), and myself were the only ones he genuinely loved back. "He was always nice to me," said Cille. I knew what she meant. She was still alive...

Besides, as it turned out, I had even underestimated him in death. It took all three of us, using Ira's truck, to get him to his grave. We lowered him in, and each of us threw in a handful of dirt. After that, I insisted on filling in his grave alone, which I did for the next six hours. Of all the unpleasant things I have had to do in my 55 years of existence, this was the most difficult. Knowing I would never see his beautiful face looking happily at me with those remorseless killer's eyes, was almost more than I could – and can – bear.

I will always have pets. I love dogs, cats, and for that matter, most of God's creatures (OK – rats and spiders I can do without), but there can never be another Lazarus the Wolf. He was unique. He was of a breed of animal that had been, until Man's slaughter had begun, one of the mightiest predators – truly, a perfect killing machine – that ever walked the North American continent. In the end, it became apparent that his love had overcome even his instincts – a true testament to the power of love.

The Lord has blessed me in many ways over the years, but having Laz's love was really and truly the greatest gift I have ever received. If there is a heaven – and I hope to God there is – I know I have to be good, because Lazarus is waiting there for me. Except this time, there will be no fences, no worries, just eternal love.

Post Script

Having written this story, it is my hope that the reader will *not* be encouraged to possess a hybrid or full-blooded wolf. It is also my hope that while the reader understands the amazing bond that existed between Lazarus and myself, they should also understand that wolves do not belong in the home. Nor do they belong in populated areas. The best place for wolves now, is certainly not the home, or even the continental United States. It is Alaska, and other such remote places. It is not fair to the wolves to relocate them here in the States.

Regardless of what the legislation is, the reality is that people will shoot them, justified or not.

I was lucky in that my relationship with Lazarus was a safe one, but it was more coincidence and circumspection than anything else. Had I gotten him when he was an adult and did not know his history, the end to my story could have been very different. He was unique and there is no chance that the situation could be ever duplicated.

In other words, beware, my friends. Wolves are not evil, but they are dangerous beyond anything you can imagine. They are magnificent creatures who belong in the wild places, as God intended – not your living room.

Drew Gomber
Lincoln, New Mexico
September, 2004

ABOUT THE AUTHOR

Drew Gomber is a freelance writer for the *Ruidoso News* and lives in Lincoln, with his animals. Drew is the author of "Lincoln County War: Heroes and Villains" "Past Tense: American Souls, Vol. I" and "The Lincoln County War: A Primer".

Drew is also known for his television advisory work with the History Channel on their "Wild West Tech" Series and the "Billy the Kid Unmasked" special for the Discovery Channel, as well as numerous other radio and television appearances.

www.ingramcontent.com/pod-product-compliance
Lightning Source LLC
Chambersburg PA
CBHW060724030426
42337CB00017B/3006